2025 FACTS FOR

SMART KIDS

BY

MIKE AWRAK

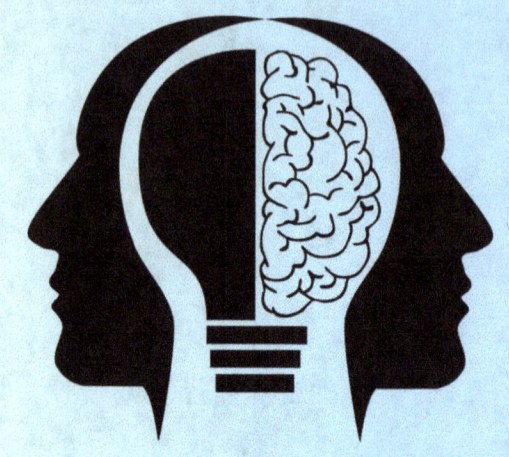

THIS BOOK BELONGS TO

_____

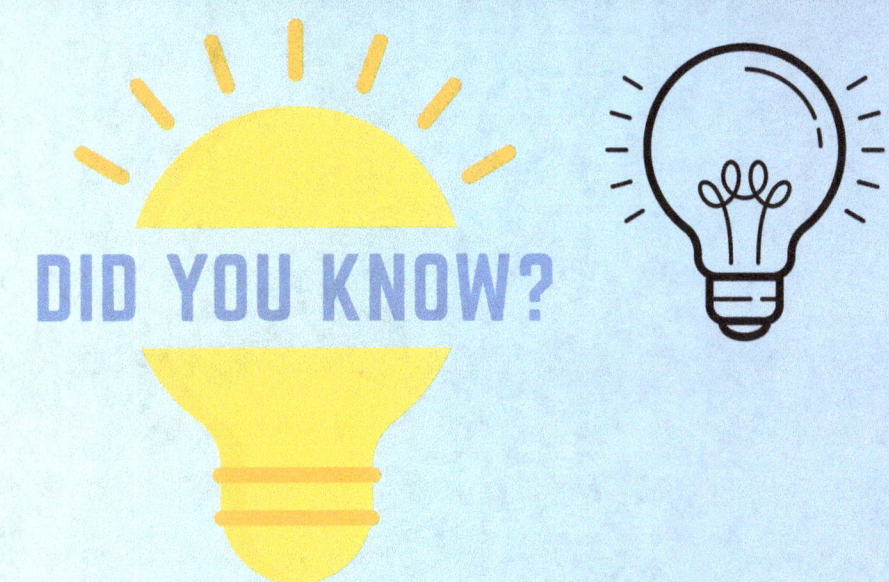

DID YOU KNOW?

FOR THE KIDS WHO LOVES FACTS

ISBN: 979-8-89458-206-1

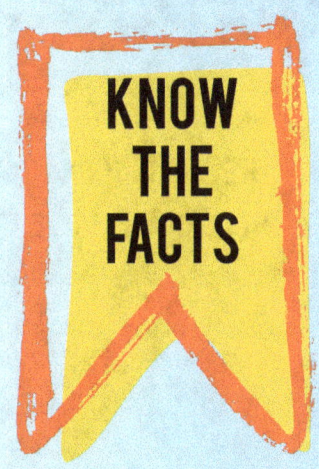

KNOW
THE
FACTS

DID YOU KNOW? THE SUN IS SO BIG THAT 1.3 MILLION EARTHS CAN FIT INSIDE IT!

WOW FACT! OCTOPUSES HAVE THREE HEARTS, AND THEIR BLOOD IS BLUE. ISN'T THAT COOL?

GUESS WHAT? SOME PLANTS EAT BUGS TO SURVIVE, LIKE THE
VENUS FLYTRAP!

AMAZING! SHARKS LIVED BEFORE DINOSAURS—MORE THAN 400 MILLION YEARS AGO.

SUPER SURPRISING! BANANAS ARE BERRIES, BUT STRAWBERRIES ARE NOT!

UNBELIEVABLE! THERE ARE MORE STARS IN SPACE THAN GRAINS OF SAND ON EARTH.

FUN FACT! SLOTHS ARE SO SLOW THAT ALGAE GROWS ON THEIR FUR.

MIND-BLOWING! YOUR BRAIN CAN HOLD MORE INFORMATION THAN ALL THE BOOKS IN A LIBRARY.

DID YOU KNOW? THE EIFFEL TOWER CAN GROW TALLER IN SUMMER BECAUSE METAL EXPANDS IN HEAT!

COOL FACT! BUTTERFLIES TASTE WITH THEIR FEET. IMAGINE TASTING PIZZA WITH YOUR TOES!

AMAZING! ANTS NEVER SLEEP, AND THEY CAN LIFT 50 TIMES THEIR WEIGHT.

SURPRISING! SEA OTTERS HOLD HANDS WHILE SLEEPING TO KEEP FROM DRIFTING APART.

WOW FACT! THERE'S A PLACE ON EARTH WHERE IT HASN'T RAINED IN 2 MILLION YEARS—ANTARCTICA'S DRY VALLEYS.

JELLYFISH HAVE BEEN AROUND LONGER THAN DINOSAURS
AND EVEN TREES!

DID YOU KNOW? AN OCTOPUS CAN FIT THROUGH A HOLE THE SIZE OF A COIN. IT HAS NO BONES!

FUN FACT! LIGHTNING IS HOTTER THAN THE SURFACE OF THE SUN.

THERE ARE GLOW-IN-THE-DARK MUSHROOMS IN SOME FORESTS. SPOOKY, RIGHT?

WOW FACT! A GROUP OF FLAMINGOS IS CALLED A
"FLAMBOYANCE."

DID YOU KNOW? HUMMINGBIRDS ARE THE ONLY BIRDS THAT
CAN FLY BACKWARD.

SUPER SURPRISING! POLAR BEARS' FUR IS NOT WHITE. IT'S SEE-THROUGH AND REFLECTS LIGHT.

MIND-BLOWING! THERE'S A LAKE IN AUSTRALIA THAT IS BRIGHT PINK.
IT'S CALLED LAKE HILLIER.

AMAZING! WHALES CAN SING SONGS THAT TRAVEL 1,000 MILES
UNDERWATER.

GUESS WHAT? HONEY NEVER SPOILS. SOME HONEY IS 3,000 YEARS OLD AND STILL EDIBLE!

DID YOU KNOW? THE FASTEST GUST OF WIND EVER RECORDED WAS 253 MILES PER HOUR.

COOL FACT! THE MOON HAS MOONQUAKES, JUST LIKE EARTH HAS EARTHQUAKES.

SURPRISING! STARFISH HAVE NO BRAINS BUT CAN REGROW THEIR ARMS IF THEY LOSE ONE.

MIND-BLOWING! THERE'S A JELLYFISH THAT CAN LIVE FOREVER—IT'S CALLED TURRITOPSIS DOHRNII.

FUN FACT! CAMELS' HUMPS DON'T STORE WATER—THEY STORE FAT FOR ENERGY.

WOW FACT! THE LONGEST RECORDED FLIGHT OF A CHICKEN IS 13 SECONDS.

AMAZING! SOME FROGS CAN FREEZE SOLID IN WINTER AND THAW BACK TO LIFE IN SPRING.

GUESS WHAT? RAINBOWS CAN HAPPEN AT NIGHT. THEY'RE CALLED MOONBOWS.

SUPER SURPRISING! YOU'RE TALLER IN THE MORNING THAN AT NIGHT BECAUSE YOUR SPINE COMPRESSES DURING THE DAY.

FUN ACTIVITY
COLORING

YOUR ACTIVITY IS TO COLOR THE ROBOTS AND NAME THEM IN THE NEXT FEW PAGES AND SHARE IT WITH YOUT FRIENDS.

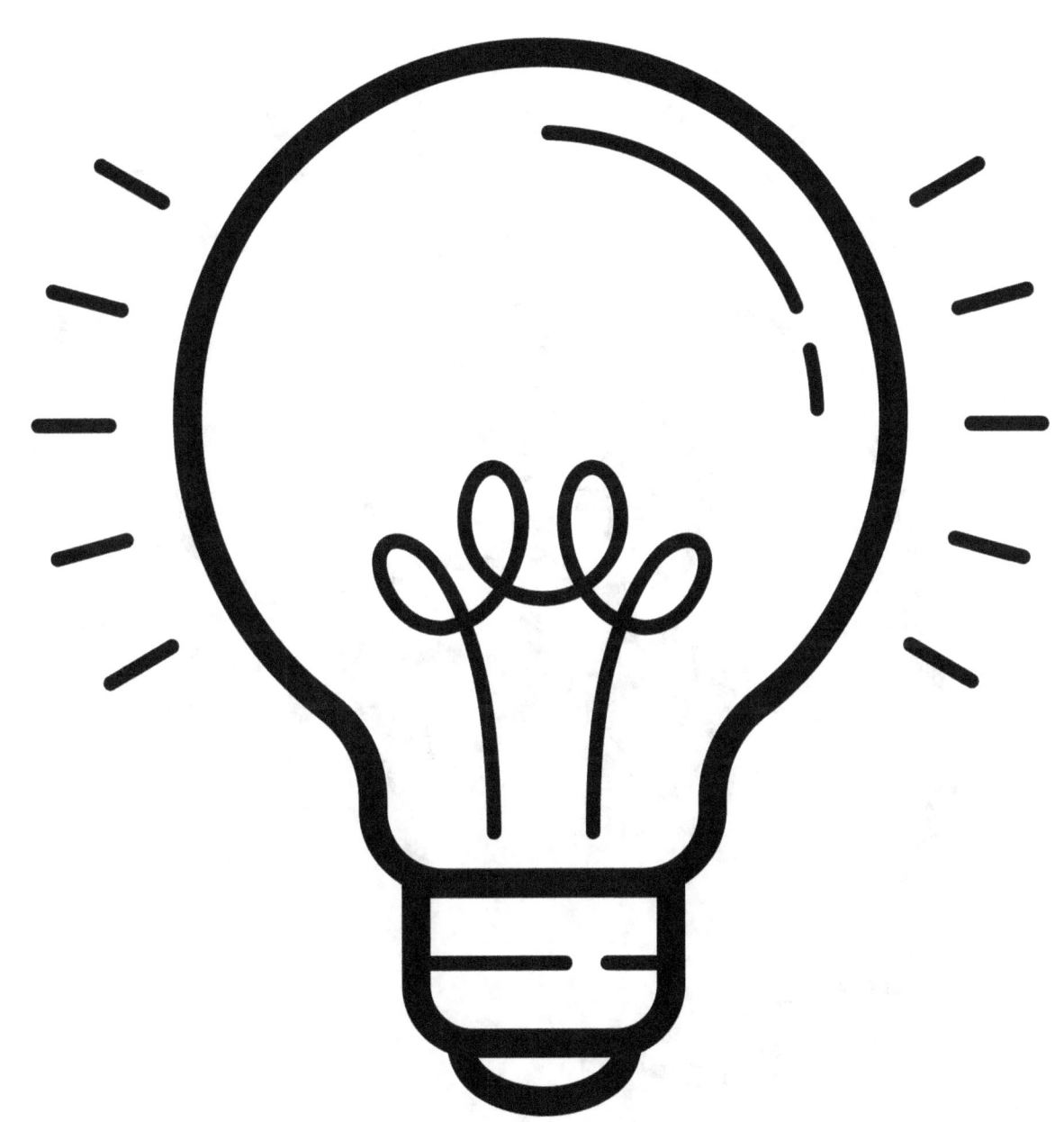

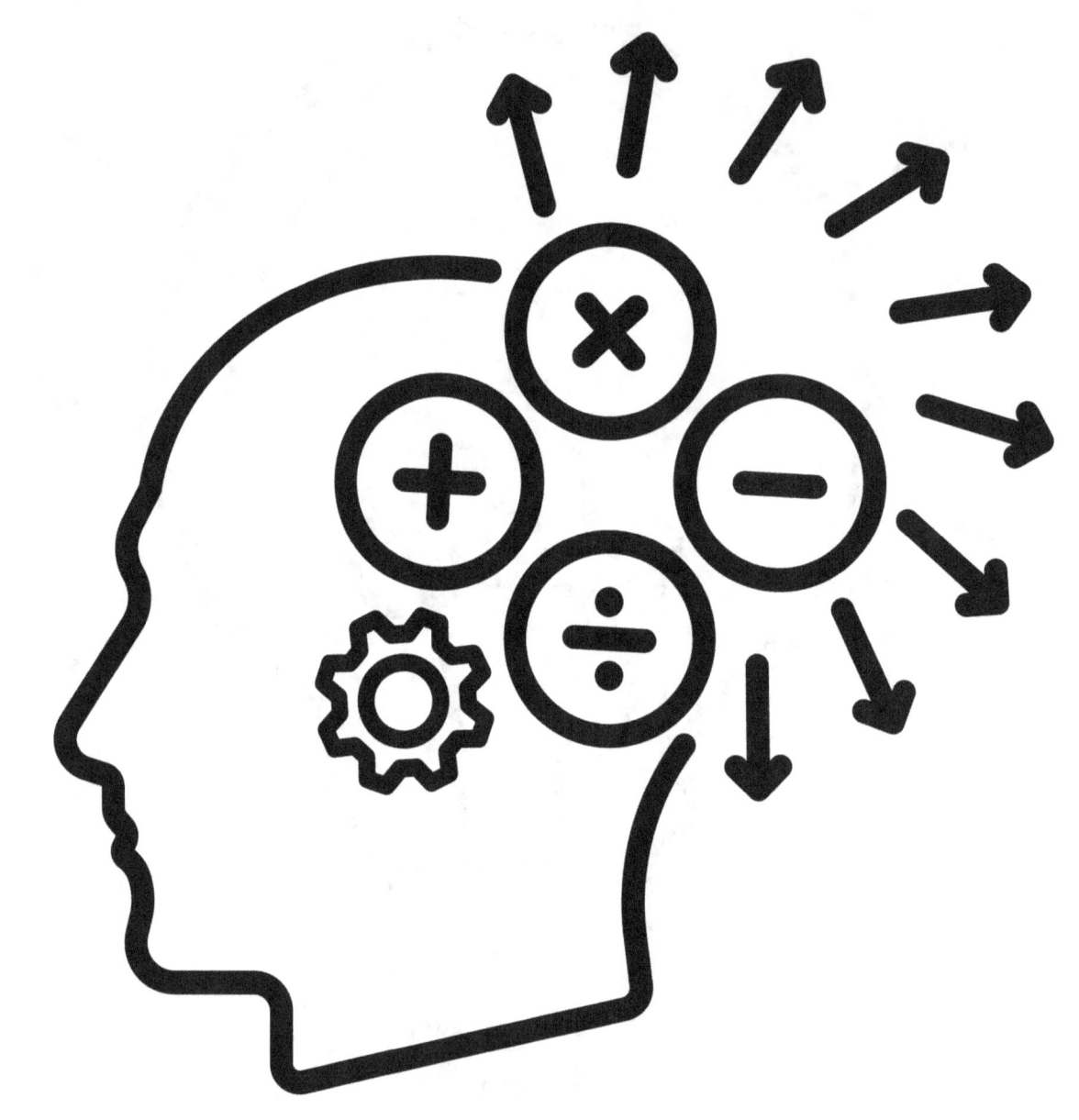

DID YOU KNOW?

FACT

I HOPE YOU LIKED THIS BOOK. PLEASE CHECK OUT MY OTHER BOOKS

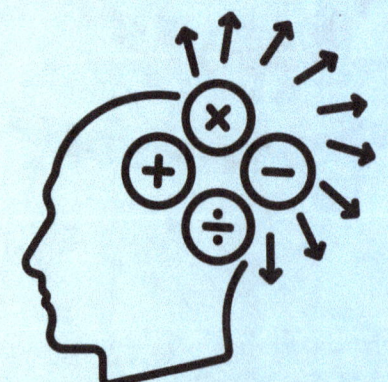